METAMORPHOSES

BOOKS BY EVAN KENNEDY

I am, am I, to trust the joy that joy is
no more or less there now than before (Roof Books, 2020)
Jerusalem Notebook (O'clock Press, 2017)
The Sissies (Futurepoem, 2016)
Terra Firmament (Krupskaya, 2013)
Shoo-Ins to Ruin (Gold Wake Press, 2011)

CITY LIGHTS SPOTLIGHT SERIES NO. 22

EVAN KENNEDY

META-
MORPHOSES

CITY LIGHTS
SAN FRANCISCO

CITY LIGHTS SPOTLIGHT
The City Lights Spotlight Series was founded in 2009,
and is edited by Garrett Caples.

Library of Congress Cataloging-in-Publication Data
Names: Kennedy, Evan, author.
Title: Metamorphoses : poetry / Evan Kennedy.
Description: San Francisco, CA : City Lights Books, 2023. |
Series: City lights spotlight ; 22
Identifiers: LCCN 2022044026 | ISBN 9780872869004 (trade paperback)
Subjects: LCGFT: Poetry.
Classification: LCC PS3611.E5595 M48 2023 | DDC 811/.6--dc23/eng/20220912
LC record available at https://lccn.loc.gov/2022044026

City Lights Books are published at the City Lights Bookstore,
261 Columbus Avenue, San Francisco, CA 94133
www.citylights.com

FOR JASON MORRIS

CONTENTS

METAMORPHOSES

...the gods don't like intruders.

ROBERTO CALASSO (TRANS. RICHARD DIXON)

Unfortunately, there are no longer any barbarians
to infuse new blood into a new faith.

SIMONE WEIL (TRANS. ARTHUR WILLS)

...Rome,—at once the Paradise,
The grave, the city, and the wilderness

PERCY BYSSHE SHELLEY

A KNIFE

cut the fish
that drank
the water
that doused
the fire
that burned
the branch
that perched
the bird
that dodged
the hand
that drafted
lyric

SAN FRANCISCO CHASE SCENE

Help! I'm being chased through this infinite city this dubious
    utopia   Pedaling my bike full-speed uphill past startup
        hells I cough and gasp, my seducer just behind me

If you ever need to escape you don't dare look back or
    even blink   My thighs burn and cramp my heart almost
        bursting when I swallow bugs splattered through

my eyes   Sure I bike fast but this creep is my equal and
    headbutts my back wheel   I steady myself then turn sharp
        on Duboce Ave. against the wind onlookers panicked

"Idiot!" "Look out!" "Hey that's a stop sign!"   My near
    collisions include a pricy stroller with overgrown toddler on
        iPad, a dog more expensive than my rent,

a pissed-off driver wearing an always tasteless LA Dodgers cap
    Weaving between cars honking for my death I yell *Help!*
        Teeth tear my ankles and calves, blood and spit flying—

Then an ecstatic blast splits this terrible scene—one of my
    household gods hears me!   Is it Bob Dylan in
        Malibu plagiarizing Juvenal? Shiva in

Omkareshwar admiring the marigolds I offered? Exiled Ovid
　　trimming his laurel crown? Or is it Franz Kafka
　　　　watching traffic through the eyes of a stray dog?

Whoever it is drops everything and with my handsome
　　spectral face in mind they ask where? when? how?
　　　　They know my name and devotion—

I slip from the pedals (a tearing sound)　　My black Converse
　　rip open from toenails made into talons　　Wings burst
　　　　from my shoulders, ruin my goddamn new black jacket,

spread and thrash the air so that a leap from my pedals
　　lifts me off my bicycle...　　In winged society, I peek through
　　　　Victorian windows, awful condos of steel and glass,

transformations of this city I love.　　I want to give thanks
　　but I've lost my elocution and boy-killing charm...
　　　　Tail feathers thrash in my pants, black denim slipping

off my legs in tatters　　Teeth lengthen fuse and sharpen: it's a
　　slender beak for my new hunger　　(Maybe it's fine?
　　　　Maybe I've outlived my life and its obsessions?)

　　　　Unacquainted with my new species
　　　　I take to the sky unthinkingly from Elgin Park
　　　　(It's the block where one of my favorite poets,
　　　　Ronald Johnson, lived...)

My failed assailant raging below me
kicking my bicycle

To me it's useless!
I won't recognize it

tomorrow   !

TREE OF LIFE

In the tree of life I lose my way
upper branches tangled vines self-reflected creation
it's not my intention to forget my origin
a sunbeam illumines me
my descendants inferiors in branches below
my own face blooming smiling cawing
I was birthed raised from below
lifted onto a branch then fell into gravity's biomass
The tree of life calls to me inscribes my lineage
ears enclose a sonic globe
beside me my contemporaries
close relations within touch while
I jump swing fly to others farther away I resemble less
Hold onto that image recite it
I wait for these branches to be canceled
entire history existent within me
my identity comprises life nothing more
my appearance is its alteration

NATURE BOY

Why is he sad of eye?
Everyone wishes to adorn nature
to feel vivisected by desire
life-exhilarated in transparent dress
revealing masked-naked wildlife—
then to be laid out on your back by pleasure!
A continual second innocence...

I'm at home scribbling verse about
how receiving his love implies violence
turning Rilke's panther into Blake's tyger
His chance moves encompass a habitat
enlivening mine through invasion
tooth filing, lip smacking, skull shaping—
opening my face with a raw grin

TO OVID

I tracked you in Rome this September where statues
your contemporaries lack arms noses cocks. Casualties of
time's war on us or changes in taste. We share atoms
with countless living and dead, missing marble limbs,
but I pursue unclaimed meat, stray unincorporated matter
moving through plumbing, open forms, atmospheres,
malls, your anonymous grave.

        Excluded, indifferent to the constant world,
you made epic the bodies split from within, faces erupting
from different species' features, new lifeforms emerging in
your darling bucolic anatomical theater, perverse as free verse.
I'm as foreign to you as articulation in the entropy I inhabit,
a barbaric language I can't understand though I'm made
its captive because I'm made of it—in elegy. I'm not pursuing
you exactly but resemblance through subjectless tissue
and muscle, expanding grim tradition to keep leopards happy
lounging in mossy temples long after belief.

WHY THE ORACLE DISAPPEARED

is unclear. His metered speech loosened,
his imagery, once perfect interplay
of instruction and symbol, soon
became so obscure that we lost
interest in studying his imprecise
pronouncements, which, approaching
the oracle's thousandth year in our village,
deteriorated into a murmur of
homonyms, split infinitives, and
cliché: a near-wordless exhalation.
Was that "pen" as in enclose or as in write?
"Wound" (woond) as in injure or
"wound" (waʊnd) as in wrapped around
the virgin standing indignantly before
that vaporous tripod, incense, sacrifice?

Perhaps people cannot tremble through
an entire millennium. Slaves, maybe.
But for delivery boys, art handlers,
immigrants, physicists, and postcard
vendors like me, it's difficult to tell.
Our uncertainty indicates the oracle
failed. At the very least, there's a crisis

(of faith? inspiration?) leading our oracle
to disappear, or at best, speak on diminished
authority. Evidence supports both theories.

Leaving the oracle, visitors report
a mishmash of gestures, riddles, etymologies,
events, negations. My ear stays tuned
to the game on the radio . . .

                             No matter
my spotless conduct, I cannot ask the oracle
to reflect on himself. Doing so might
cause our homes or, far less visibly,
our culture, which unites our community
and dialect, to explode. It's all plausible
in the so-called *navel of the world*.

TO APOLLO

"I dream of the death of the sun" —JENNIFER MOXLEY

FOR BRETT PRICE

When I say your name, Apollo, I lend you
living breath. You possess me, my body unsuited
for a deity but full of desire and contempt.
That's life enough. I prolong your existence. I lay
devotions at your feet for your work as the sun.
Creator of life, peeler of sunburns.

I drove to Nevada City after evacuation orders
lifted. Fire destroyed almost 40 homes.
It's 80% contained, they say, though as your
haphazard devotee, I know nothing contains you.
Maybe one cell of mine if anything does. Light
must be intuited within us, carried like
endorphins or vitamins. I keep naming you
to sustain me and keep death away.

I think of death only as a Romantic,
like you've fucked me in my bed, a burning
fissure, or volcano. Some friends speak of
ecological collapse, the warming that follows
our thinning defenses, but I think they're just afraid
of their death. All that talk is a stand-in.

They turned their back to Apollo, spurned
you as you hurry your approach to us.
Their world went dark. It's something I
won't let myself do, not yet. I accept
the sunburns and fires and conjugate from
my weakness an active assertion that
you, Apollo, exist and we because of you.

I fear loneliness, being misunderstood (especially
in poems), venereal disease, the collapse of
the empire where I was born. Planetary collapse
is something I hope my death will precede,
perhaps at dawn like Lou Reed staying up all night
awed by beauty as his body finished rejecting
his new liver. Long Island beauty.

Being up all night terrifies me.
Anticipating dawn's arrival, I hurry to bed.
If I try sleeping with you nearby, it's
too late to make anything of the day you give.
I want to be given many more. But seeing
you rise? Seeing dawn? No way. Absolutely not.

HELLAGABALUS RIDES AGAIN

AFTER ELAGABALUS, ROMAN EMPEROR 218–222

Bring Rome to Oakland
indica for introversion, sativa for sadism
Solar priest, twink emperor queuing at Bakesale Betty?
Instead try flamingo brain, sow udder, Lake Merritt goose liver
these lentils need more pearls more gold dust
bourgeois marxists smothered by two tons of narcissus
more pennyroyal wine, $1.92 chow mein
glass imitation fruit and pastry
single-use onyx toilets
bare-assed metalhead moshing at Full of Hell
lock up drunk friends to wake with pet leopards
baths demolished, armpits ripen   East Bay sun the only god

Hellagabalus, ride elephants in the Coliseum 7th inning stretch
hide scarlet silk nooses from the devastated A's

JOHN DONNE AND OTHER MATING HABITS

1. The Second Flea

It sucked you and now me,
not only this flea—
              my chest hair's lice,
      the fungus constellating
                    across your breasts
    a wandering crab
            preferring your crotch
        to mine   (a complement I verified)

I decline antibiotics to
      feel fully bacteria
              bred from our sex
                  burning pangs of birth for
          those too small for sight
                    in our skin and discharge

Mine is not just a slut's homage
      or host's warm welcome

It's the intuited expansion of life,

              facing execution by your fingernail
              and spared as long as I'm watchful

2. Aubade

In bed she and I are   antidote for the biomass
    but she complains   it's already dawn

I'll later write:
   "Why should we rise?
             Because it's light?"
but now I growl "Sun, back off:
      I feel fucked senseless, content,
        I won't bathe again"

  aubade   unlocking my jaw
I blink in amplexus   hours making days
     while suckers encircle the bedpost
        apricot branch grafted onto peach

       my desire indifferent to threat
          or dismemberment

3. Valediction

Scratching my name on
    her windowpane
  I disappear down Regent Street
   damp with dawn-lit dewfall
 taste of her snatch on my lips

Only love me in plurality—
    I am oath and honesty

  All attract their destruction
    ears independent from will

  Afternoon arrives by its own force
    I switch from shade of chestnut
      to fig tree as the sun
        and my reading progress

Draw a bath   encircle me
  membrane surrounding hatchlings

SEDUCING MY READER

For you it's a rotten fish
  I rolled in to
demonstrate time
    bundling prey silky
    when worse poets
offer decoys in
    faddish language

  My singing
   slickens canopy nests
spotted by eyes
  waking gardens'
    blind sensation

I blush watching
   you read me
Put down my book so
I can approach and pulsate
  with experience and
            observation

WHY MADONNA IS NOT IN MY PANTHEON

I was kicked out of her concert   I'm still so ashamed
I snuck from the balcony to the floor and touched
her (just lightly) when she danced up the aisle:
     her shoulders spanned my two hands.
The next day I told Bruce how I lost control and
my wallet when her bodyguards 86'ed me
       Oh, and Madonna's really tiny!
Bruce like a classicist said "She must be from southern Italy."

I feel like young Ovid on his worst day—
Madonna was breathtakingly beautiful even vulnerable.
   Couture black lace blouse, wig of taut brown curls
It affirmed my love for her though not as I would like
   She's only the richest person I've touched.
     She's not even in my pantheon anymore.

TO ATTIS

Just as you, Attis, swear devotion to Magna Mater—
the great mother!—I follow several: Judy Garland,
Mary Beard, Tori Amos, Lisa Jarnot, Alice Notley,
Yuja Wang, Jackqueline Frost, Simone Weil, a few others
                    a vision out of Christine de Pizan

Brilliant as they are they cannot solve all my problems,
but Attis, spare me the suggestion I do as you did.
Why must you and fellow worshippers castrate
yourselves, cut open your arms and shoulders?
Why dance wildly around a sacred pine whipping
yourselves knucklebones beating timbrels
and pine cones lacerating bare chests splattering tree
and altar with sweat and gore then why apply gold leaf
to your freshly wounded genitals?
            To imitate harvest
                    in human inclination toward the eternal. . .
            To throw yourself
                    before a woman who will not reject your desire.
Like you I propagate nothing but lyric.

Attis, you'd agree with graffiti from Imperial Rome:
            Baths, wine, and sex ruin our bodies
            but make life worth living.

By that standard I've lived far beyond my 37 years—
I suffer a million sorrows, yet
the thought of your severed balls hitting the dirt—
two dull thuds—makes me shudder, puts an ache in mine.
Two jocks I went to college with called theirs *evil brains*

Attis, tell me how to stop hating on poets, gawking at
their selfishness, defilement by ambition, sex lives,
careerism, countless moral failings, posing as Marxists
while bankrupting students, ruining friendships
so that I fear trusting friends who write.

Deliver me from the despair of Jack Spicer, Weldon Kees,
Landis Everson, John Wieners, Steve Abbott, Sam D'Allesandro
(If these names are unfamiliar, substitute them with
those like you (same city and obsessions) who died too soon.)

Augustine was disgusted by your followers, their
"hair moist with perfume, faces made-up,
limbs flaccid, walk effeminate, wandering through
Carthage demanding people subsidize their
shameful life"   while a critic calls Judy Garland's fans
a flutter of fags   trunks full of roses dragged
into New York's Palace Theater   It all alters my body
as leaden weights are snipped to free me from
terrestrial restrictions extending my limbs seraphic
broadening my chest loosening me from gravity so

that my voice reaches empyrean registers
a note sustained over 60 seconds captivating an
audience who had stopped holding their breath
 Like fans of castrati said *Death is in your throat*

Attis, not all Americans think you're crazy.
Do (as in "dough"), leader of Heaven's Gate,
has wet dreams about a devotee, a young actor from L.A. Listen,
I get it. For an L.A. boy I'd crawl from Melrose to Echo Park
whimpering outside his building and texting *Why no reply?*

To become solitary Ovid in early 21st century
imperial decline—sure, I'll play *that* role, but
communal living? No way, that's not for me!
It occurs to Do that the "bodily vehicle" requires customizing.
Nodding along to his plan, a flurry of suck-ups bicker over
who deserves to lose their evil brains first.
 They didn't know you, Attis, but in a sense became
your devotees, receiving brand-new Nikes
before eating applesauce laced with phenobarbital, tying plastic
bags over their heads, and ascending into space.
As they joked, *Just* Do *it.*
   Nike: winged goddess of victory

Late one night in the dorm I heard the jocks laughing about
pissing in someone's shampoo Mystery solved:
earlier I was lathering my scalp with feeble liquidy bubbles

and suspected the shower head dripped into the bottle.
What's worse than my false hypothesis? The jocks
were cute, I took retroactive pleasure: regret's antithesis

Each Magna Mater circles me
Their poems texts lyrics fill the flaw I was born into
Attis, make me good in my bodily vehicle
                                    but not yet

LIFE DRAWING

I am a portrait sketched by an ape
    depicting what time will make of her

Veins and bones   nerves and guts
    arms pelvis legs of course my blue eyes

        Around her feet (my mother's)   abandoned studies
        a continuum of forms

LIFE PROPAGANDA

You're looking to go where? The map of
my nervous system is transposable to the terrain or water you cross
I wave to you and my arm unrolls a spool or scroll
I rather the sense of smell vacate my snout than the suck to leave
    my arms
I rather the scarlet markings leave my petals than my egg pouch
    tear
I'll ever be your beast of burden
I'll draw pull coax melodies from your tongue because it's
    slickened every inch of me

Substituting myself letter for cell
No need to read the message it spells
Tablet on a walk   Cup speaking its contents

You and I are captive to a degree
Suspended mid-metamorphosis
Souls' limbo   way station   brackish outpost

                Petals no they're eyelids I open

MY OWN VERSION OF YOU

I make my own version of you
from the one who starts out a poor agrarian boy in trouble with the
    cops
who wears a sequined apron
who hears my first good poem then kisses my cheek
whose forehead grows horns
who attempts emerging from darkness through the presumption of
    dawn
who is the face of Masala Munch
who gives reasons why things look as they do
who refuses his sorrow to turn to hate
who hangs a small plastic Hanuman from his sail
who takes part in the life of a sparrow visiting his window
who endorses body sprays and beard trimmers for gents to "look
    fresh"
who thanks to Isis is transformed from a donkey back to a man
who first encountering her signature song asks, "What does 'pastoral'
    mean?"
who is forced into imagination and self-observation
who perfects wireless electricity at 46 and 48 East Houston Street
who loosens self from gravity
who requests substitutions when ordering a Cobb salad

whose corpse is identified by the books in his pockets

who begins "Raining Blood" with ominous drums

who is lost in Rome, contemplates suicide, then is dissuaded by
    voices he last heard in childhood

whose skull resonates with song

who authors *The Antidote*

who turns her head in imitation of the sun

whose poet get-together loses all cheer (Stalin on the phone)

who disguises himself as Hermes to serve as psychopomp

whose garlanded donkey intuits the gospel

whose spirit journey requires he clings hard to a speeding cloud

who invokes the dog that's got no master

who notifies a MoMA security guard that their Matisse is
    upside-down

who sings not quite as divinely as Roy Orbison but is exponentially
    more handsome

who requests his corpse be dumped before the White House

who reads in a dictionary that he's the only cited authority for a word
    he's unsure ever existed

whose tagline, "This is the cycle of life," is a comfort in evil times

who trains racehorses immortalized on earthen lamps

who's a gentleman cricketer on a drinks break

who gives me directions to the temple of Santa Muerte

who ignites her Bösendorfer in a Florida parking lot

who organizes readings for all visiting poets

who drops his Phoenician urn and trembles before Boeotia's serpent

who instructs his session players, "Go for whatever you're hearing"
who cruises gardens, promenades, stadia, and toilets
who sings "Somewhere Over the Rainbow" in my sadness
who is my sister in spiritual delinquency
who plants serpent teeth and harvests men in armor
whose heart resists cremation
who envisions a brigade of nurses parachuting behind enemy lines
who covers his forehead in ash
who through friendship confirms the gospel of Christ
who when dying hands over his water and explains, "Your need is
    greater than mine"
who boops the snoot
who kisses me on the lips after his concert at The Masonic and says,
    "You're a good boy"
who's stunned to see a young shepherd draw a perfect circle
who tours Europe dancing around teepees with Buffalo Bill's Wild
    West Show
who introduces the saxophone to Ethiopia
who sings within its egg before hatching
who wants to fuck me like an animal
who tells friends that in Greece they'll be sane
who believes there is nothing like fine weather, and health, and
    Books, and a fine country, and a contented mind, and Diligent-
    habit of reading and thinking, and an amulet against the ennui
who works as an umbrella holder and in downtime writes poems to
    Shiva

who assists excavations by Prince Giovanni Torlonia

who acknowledges that baths, wine, and sex ruin our bodies but
    make life itself

who seeks a world as beautiful as his wardrobe

whose sexual charisma catalyzes societal collapse

who says she'd be a great Supreme Court justice because she's always
    been judgmental

who's fairest among hills and vales

who meeting Queen Victoria likens her to an approaching fire but
    enjoys his visit

who finds a moment of mercy in Tomis

who walks into the blade-like arms of God

MY MINOTAUR

My lineage was mutilated. My father was as certain of his power as he was my intelligence (a monster's). In my labyrinth's center (a lair) I hit puberty and confusion. I intuited the outside (a world) animating my limbs and lifting my ears.

From instinct (my enigma) I tested hypotheses about the world withdrawn from mine. I improvised dramas for no other audience than damp breezes from obstructed vistas (I intuited a sea.). I made my own popular culture. Art amazed me: affection or terror out from nothing. I knew no other animal. The labyrinth's scale suggested a crazy nation or clear-eyed architect. I felt it reach from within me to console me then other times grab my throat.

Once I punched a hole through the northeast wall. (This was before I proved this area was a decoy (Shouldn't I say "all but proved" to delay the humiliation of having wasted months (What if my turns replicated in the west opened a view onto the sea (emergence from the labyrinth and its maker's brain)?)?).)

A void or vista. That's what the minotaur-fist-shaped hole resembled. I responded by escaping to my center (my trusty lair) and shelving my plan. My maps (scratched onto leaves blown into my enclosure) were sequenced in reverse chronology then stored in a fissure that recently opened at my lair's western entry.

My surrender was all-encompassing. Consider that I saw the fissure as storage but missed that my labyrinth without a keeper was falling apart. I was too bored to follow its decline. Instinct and labyrinth (unlikely conspirators) alerted me of threats but I did nothing like fortifying walls or sleeping in a different corner. If I couldn't respond to instincts coded within me (forget I was first of my species) would I ever find a companion or even survive? My dream of revenge weakened to resentment and mistrust of my body.

No longer attempting to escape I almost floated above my labyrinth. Soon after (or years later) I looked up and no question with my horns before me my labyrinth would collapse under any direction I walked. I developed (again from intuition) a distant idea. In a language not only I created I would explain my innocence. (To whom? To them. And those like me.)

PHAETHON AND THE CONSTELLATIONS

I don't know what neurons begin firing when
I try to talk like the galaxy I occupy:

Kid loses control of sun's chariot   flames
sweep through space   orbits unfetter   we fall into
each other   each star unfixing   every
claw belt fin horn mane hoof of ours disbanding. . .
I am drifting spinning burning
swinging around alien axes as what was my horn
gores you before you change shape   globular clusters
crowning a fish's head winging other
illogical pairings until the correspondences between
shape and symbol   our only language   fail. . .

We forget our names racing through and
extending equinoxes seasons   a contraction or spasm
through burgeoning decimation   a blossom
eliminating equators   a tear distended over boiling seas
Time inoperative in torn orbit   meteorologists' disbelief

KEATS ROUTINES

The cockney poet
    "hoisted himself dominant"
like the sea-shouldering
    whale "gaping for
sustenance" with
    "capacious mouth" like
    newborn birds
"dabbling his forepaws
hither and tither" like a
    baited bear spinning
from his mind
    a spider's "airy Citadel" of
verse then took part
    in the life of a sparrow
pecking at his window
    as he convalesced

ROMANTIC MAYHEM

You call me dead but I say not yet
Breezes make an inland sea of our superblooming meadow
such is Romanticism's intellectual expanse
poppy anemone dogwood narcissus
primeval lightscape swept with mist breath vapor scent
interchanging colors exceeding eyesight's spectrum

                    a galaxy in earthy clod
                    sentient with living memory

                         •

I get it now—you mean I'm Dead,
vocalist of black metal band Mayhem
When I was Dead I belonged in the woods where
I buried my clothes then exhumed them for concerts in
Zeitz Leipzig Jessheim Sarpsborg
embellished with asphodel cinquefoil red clover impatiens

We are as clouds that veil the midnight moon
                              (wrote Shelley)
When it's cold and dark the freezing moon can obsess you
                              (Dead sang)

                         •

A test of contrasts—Dead me and abundant rioting blooms
April 1991: Dead, wearing his I ♥ Transylvania shirt, is found
slumped beside his shotgun, skull blasted
("Excuse the blood but I have slit my wrists and neck")

My brain—"shelter to imagination's demesne"—
rests in my arms on willow laurel lilac crocus lavender
propagating themselves from out my open memory

honesty   heart's ease

WHAT WE'RE GOING ON WITH

In a species whose migration
    exceeds the lifespan of the individual
        each of us presumes discontinuity
    a culture and way of life
        shaped through incomplete acts
    intuited through instinct or education

THIS IS MY OVIDIAN COURSE

Ovid begins his Amores by reporting a theft: Cupid stole a metrical foot from his heroic line! It leaves him no choice but to write elegy: the form of frustrated desire.

Heroic couplet: — ˘ ˘ | — ˘ ˘ | — ˘ ˘ | — ˘ ˘ | — ˘ ˘ | — ˘

— ˘ ˘ | — ˘ ˘ | — ˘ ˘ | — ˘ ˘ | — ˘ ˘ | — ˘

Elegiac couplet: — ˘ ˘ | — ˘ ˘ | — ˘ ˘ | — ˘ ˘ | — ˘ ˘ | — ˘

— ˘ ˘ | — ˘ ˘ | — | — ˘ ˘ | — ˘ ˘ | —

Amputating this foot creates a hobble or hesitation seen more in arrow-struck romantics than epic warriors. You see, Ovid is impossibly young and brilliant but berserk with lust, a pickup artist under night's cover giving women lip service.

I, too, have been that slut speaking homage, but I lack Ovid's servitude to Cupid. Roma is amor in reverse, sure, but San Francisco is looser and impulsive.

Ovid embodies urbanity, irony, snobbery—he turns up his nose until it nestles virtually anywhere on a woman's body. That nose dominates his name—Publius Ovidius *Naso*—and since he's writing elegiac meter, he must go by Naso to make it fit.

Two millennia between us, Mr. Big Nose declines my advances to cruise theaters, colonnades, racetracks, porticos. Naso occupies a time when a poet did not portray himself as a good person. He hits Corinna (who may not have ever existed) then begs her to retaliate. After her attempt to abort their baby leaves her deathly ill, he prays to Isis: Save Corinna, let her go unpunished—but not if she tries that again.

Then women reply once *Heroides* gives voice to Dido, Medea, Helen, women who "provided oars you used to leave me," who "want to be among wild beasts," who tell a lover "you cannot escape your features," conceding that a man's beauty prefigures doom.

Names desire affiliation. *Carmen perpetuum*—continual song—links *Metamorphoses*' myths-in-myths, deities' terrorism, genomic revisions explaining origins of our world and its living and inanimate occupants.

Ovid's compassion erodes the divisions between human and animal and plant, but that doesn't imply he unites them into a peaceable kingdom. What happens to the residual meat, unaddressed viscera, redundant bulk declined by the newly metamorphosed? Skin peels off in sheets, muscle unravels into damp string, bones' atoms unbind then dust springtime's blooms a dull gray, worthless as anonymous cremains. Or in the other direction: a being expands in mass, attracting environs' atoms into the density of a laurel tree or large rock where ships wreck.

Anatomy is destiny. No living thing has a single absolute voice. Every new form reenacts the error or sorrow or disaster that catalyzed transformation. One's past self springs forward like a reflex or spasm: a shadow of a previous existence.

With an edit for a poem in mind, I return to my desk. I was only away for a minute, but the wildlife I'd been describing chewed up my notebook and pens. I turn around and laugh—"Gotcha." They're wide-eyed and motionless in the corner, puzzled, stunned to see me: possums, geckos, foxes, giraffes, octopi, their faces splattered with blue and black ink.

I undress when I see them doubt my existence. Lucky for me, I've been cutting the confetti for the day I make a wildlife sanctuary of my body.

Ovid directs us from Earth's corners into the empyrean, though he went farther, banished at 50 by Augustus to a settlement by the Black Sea: "the last outback at the world's end." We don't exactly know why. Ovid complains it's due to "a poem and an error." He composes an epic in the region's Greek patois and recites it to the locals. In return, they train him to help defend their village from barbarian invaders. At last, Ovid is a warrior.

He eventually concedes, "Though I loathe your land, you I love."

TREE OF LIFE

In the tree of life I adorn each branch with speech and action
When unaccompanied I can't even adorn the gate of the tree's
    enclosure
that boundary of corpses and debris
When outside of life my adorning is transitory whisked away
    trampled and bled
I lift an ear or whatever is receptive
A cry is transcribed in my adorning
or a fire or flood visible through branches plumage foliage
Serve life, I intoned
I'm encouraged through speech gestures grunts looks
"What kind of a . . . ?" "What reason for you . . . ?" "Why do you
    look . . . ?"
Voice reveals anatomy a form circulated by speech
I observe I experience but not at the same time
purification exhaustion rest apprehension defilement
anxiety concentration forgery doubt excitement union
I am a small gray fox carrying an infinitesimally small artifact
from the body of Ludwig Wittgenstein

JUDY GARLAND FACING EXTINCTION

I've made more comebacks than a revolving door
my stage is no larger than my shoe size
my legs have been likened to a couplet by Pope
a song I sing is a question or quest
it's a mystery what happens to my audience
the ins who applaud first and later the squares
I swallow the world if song won't erupt from my mouth

a trickle of blood down my inner thigh
life is crowning
a newborn macaque clings to my side
I cross green hills and out of me bursts a lamb
or a species thought extinct breathes once again and
    glistens with afterbirth
I'm a blushing bride in immaculate white being wed to a
    blue whale
from holocene to post-anthropocene
in salt flats my lacquered hair falls like I'm a Neanderthal
I bite through the umbilical cord of my tiny ibex
my axolotl hatchlings in gravelly banks
after my foal arrives stillborn I circle it repeatedly
I embody a library of genomes a life for the living
I lay eggs in my nest of tinsel and plastic straws

my brood shelters in your rubble

your hazmat suits are paper mâché to me

I defend the riotous varieties of life imprinting on me as
    mother

only Toto was paid less than me

a bat flutters before my mouth in my efforts of repopulating

remember the scimitar, horned oryx,

northern white-cheeked gibbon, Père David's deer

I offer wilderness to creation and watch its captive
    tranquility vanish

I suck up my young when predators approach

I eat the afterbirth leaving no trace

all my children recognize me

the boys in lavender their arms full of roses

the toads hatching from holes in my back

every moment I'm birthing and abandoned newly born

I settle for a gown of bark and moss

dried husks with some wire for a brassiere

when the light hits me I don't feel a thing

because I sing not speak

    life arrives to your understanding

BASHO EN ROUTE TO FUKUSHIMA

glowing   humid   cloudy gray film   a gateway in
   altitude's thin snowy air   forests of error meet
shuttered shrines   second to second
            peaks collapse   rivers jump   pines die

 Basho walks from pool to pool seeking water iris
        deep red-violet standards   white falls
 his notebook discloses his wish on clear nights
         to see the moon from elsewhere

 overcoat and lunch basket stained from walks through
bellflower   valerian   pampas grass   bush clover

LEOPARDS IN BOMBAY

said, "We want to begin again here, away from runaway glaciers, reef system doomsday, spray-painted polar bears, alligators in sewers, acidic oceans, colony collapse, the passenger pigeon, Tasmanian tiger, carbon supercharge, famine migration, wet markets, tear duct harvesting, microbe mega death, mass dolphin beaching, Asian termite, gypsy moth, stratospheric injection, artificial upwelling, wolves in Chernobyl, in situ burning, N95s, the dodo, the moa, sea forest heat waves, isotope gardens, invasive octopi, missions to Mars, Himalayan lilies, hermit crabs wearing Coke cans, starfish limb loss, skeletons in florescent parkas, solar system model in the stomach of a whale, spy robot meerkats, breathing sepulchers, the auk, the quagga, influenza in icebergs, mirrors in space, more migrants than subjects of Ancient Rome, evolution reset, plastic digestion, self-immolation, emerald elm beetle, zebra mussel, eighth continent theory, creepy-crawlies, shamans in condos, illegal clearances, everyday chaos, ruin reversion."

Then tipping over a clay pot of milk (a lot like our house cats), the leopards of Bombay took a deep breath and said, "

(But here our account breaks off.)

THE SEVEN SLEEPERS

I'm done for, I'm ruined, I'm toast! I misremembered the story of the Seven Sleepers. At tonight's recitation, I said they were pagans who went hunting, fell in a cave, and woke centuries later. Exhilarated to be alive, they danced hooting and hollering back to their hometown. Their gratitude transformed the dreary suburb into paradise.

If their filthy outdated clothes didn't bewilder the locals, what the Sleepers said did: "We're your ancestors." The locals replied, "Haha, what? How? You're younger than us!" But the resemblance was undeniable. Each of the Seven Sleepers had a counterpart in town: same birthmark or lisp or nervous demeanor, characteristics that almost make us unique.

(In another time, I, too, must have a counterpart. He's in Rome feeling handsome and spectral, and with no place for shade, he speeds through his itinerary and arrives at flattened sunlit ruins like a dazzling stranger.)

Tonight, before 80,000 in the Coliseum, I recited terribly inaccurately that despite the tense mood, the Seven Sleepers told their descendants it's a good idea to give thanks. They'd gathered narcissus and chrysanthemum to wrap around a young bull's budding horns. They'd lay traps for birds to sacrifice.

Too far into my narrative to be corrected, I said the Sleeper with the Nervous Look saw that the temples' reliefs of Apollo and Diana had been mutilated. Niches he'd venerated centuries earlier were emptied of their robust marble deities. I described how the Seven Sleepers lowered their eyes before they could spot on top the temples the imposing, almost immaterial, crosses that had triumphed over them.

Several hours into my recitation, I was dragged offstage. Instead of the kisses of adulation a recitation artist should expect, I got slapped across my mouth. It turns out the Seven Sleepers were Christians. When they returned to their village, they learned their descendants had kept that faith and eliminated all dissenters.

Officials in-the-know said, "You passed off a perverse variation of the perfected, artificial myth whose syllables had been preserved for centuries." It's not the Seven Sleepers who are ruined—I am, it's the end for me. The story, a lesson, had been entrusted to me. Our society survives on poetry alone. I've been celebrated nationwide for my flawless recitations, and now you rivals will sniff around this evening's transcription for my fatal flaw. It's an error I must have intended. You're welcome.

Tonight I was given the burden of a solitary dreamer, a twin I'm becoming, a new start hand-in-hand with memory and imagination, since I'm beginning to like them, my Sleepers, like I'm becoming the eighth. I wonder where we'll escape under cover of the night.

I'VE BEEN ANIMALS

I've slept under the eyes of mountain ranges and ocean depths
I've been complimented on my school brood cauldron and pounce
I've caught mice that keep Kafka awake
I've suckled twins who establish an empire
I've destroyed the robot imposter that enters my territory
I've begged tourists for snacks and friendly scratches behind my
    antlers
I've stormed the Prado and flown endlessly before the Goyas
I've preened myself until the sky goes gray and I turn to glass
I've glided low and parallel to rivers
I've been defended by my gaggle pod pack gang murder clutter
    caravan pod conspiracy quiver zeal herd cackle shadow and pride
I've even had other species answer when calling for a mate
I've failed to recognize Dionysus so he turned me into a dolphin
I've regurgitated mango to resuscitate a wasp
I've drunk from the corner of a human eye
I've lifted my snout above the pit
I've eaten fetuses then napped in dead leaves
I've hopped a magic mountain's bright vermillion boulders
I've rubbed noses in cul-de-sacs off tight damp tunnels
I've been rejected from my herd in blazing salt flats

I've felt the shape of my bones under my scales plumes pelt

I've been out in front of a dozen dead oceans

I've greeted humankind as its distant predecessor strange and exiled

I've dropped from my claws the stupid meteorite you worship

I've been metamorphosed and hunted by the dogs I trained

I've landed on the face of your messiah in anguish

I've been lassoed and bound when elsewhere I'm so revered no driver
     dares honk at me

I've stared down Thoreau who likens my head to a mix of squirrel
     and bear

I've dragged a slice of pizza into the 2nd Avenue F train tunnel

I've hijacked my host from its inside and led it wherever I want

I've been flipped around and sheared by that hick more than I would
     like to admit

I've played dead and admired the living

I've tasted an apple unfinished by Hervé Guibert dying of AIDS

I've nested in streets of radioactive waste branches vines

I've sung at your ears' upper limit

I've grunted and squealed over Shelley's recitation

I've lead processions wearing the mask of my ancestor Anubis

I've sung to be heard by exiled Ovid (he stopped writing)

I've not yet won you so what is this worth

ONE EATS WHILE THE OTHER WATCHES

Our souls are two crows
observing us from a branch.

Meanwhile
swelling-receding in lifeforms embryos stillborns carrion
we're recomposing each other transcribing reciting dripping to roots
my body dispersed reformulated by others
my insides turn to foliage a riot of blooms while mine become a
    poet's
we reach the moment where we can't remember whose mouth these
    words are coming from
the words encouraging us to life originating us in this tree

                                    •

One bird (a crow for now) has
a belief in everything
even the invisible
The other has
libidinous syntax
and a nervous lump in its throat

They might only be breathing to
select the contours of our destruction

Call it perfect disarray
dispersing the origin we reenter
a thread through every existence

·

Knowing so, provided that life lasts,
a diffusion of light through land-, sea-, and spacescapes

·

space turning
upon itself

disputable unity
void into void

neutral waves
constellate species

CAN WE BE THE NEW SPECIES?

We cycle through routines, our eyes
inhale each image of oxygen, select
the contours of our destruction-preservation,
opening holes in us, passages.

We're like two snakes twining

                    genomes' helix

TO SHIVA

FOR ZEESHAN AHMED

lord white as jasmine, which hand of yours destroys
and which saves?
                            Twirling you rotate the Earth
blurring limbs matted hair four spinning arms
a foot raised encircling matter and its opposite

America destroys without having heard of you.
We're the envy and fear of the world.
"This year destroyers will be destroyed . . ."
Did you say that or was it us Americans?

Shiva, I of course have heard of you!
Mine is a devotional poem spoken to your ever-changing forms
whether you're mass   energy   space   time
breaking ego's back

Shiva preserve our lives
preserve Honey my heartbroken teenage
Uber auto-rickshaw driver
When I answered where I came from
(funny I didn't say San Francisco)

he brightened, grinning in the rearview mirror:
"Omkareshwar! That's where my god lives!" meaning you
on your island shaped like the word *Om*

Honey asks a few questions and soon I
reluctantly confirm my god is Jesus
      (that stripped humiliated Galilean,
        a contemporary of Ovid)
If a tourist told me they just came from Houston or
Miami   Roswell or even Joshua Tree
I couldn't say, "That's where Jesus lives"

Honey's problem is he has a temper especially when
drunk so his girlfriend lost patience and dumped him
He turns around to look at me
compliments my blue eyes then makes
emphatic claims he's so heartbroken he wants to die
He's looking at me more than the road
"Look out, Honey!" I yell
Shiva I tried giving advice   I told him not to do what I do

America is shaped like no word
nothing like *love* or *fortitude*
As a child I saw in the shape of America someone sick in bed
Maine their head   Texas and Florida the bed's legs

No icon no image can contain your face or body
as no words can be read from the geography I occupy
I only see you as a blur while I'm scraping by in
destroyed places somehow preserved

How is that?   My guidebook says you dance
animating the cosmos from Omkareshwar
To get to the island I had to walk across—no joke—a replica of
the Golden Gate Bridge   Millennia separated me
from your pilgrims
I rubbed shoulders with them making me feel
like I'm Rick Steves   Michael Alig   Osip Mandelstam
To them I was *mleccha*: an Abrahamic
barbarian, curious, idiotic
I was in disbelief walking across my hometown's
bridge but none of the locals believed me
"Look it up" I said   typical American tourist

Because Omkareshwar is
your home I think of American homes
an oval bathroom mirror where
you admire yourself spinning perfuming yourself and
doing nothing with your matted hair then
a garage with tools blowtorches machetes
shears chainsaws fertilizer insecticide then
a living room where on a flatscreen you watch
Virat Kohli the cricket player who's my ideal

(as Zeeshan often teases me) then kitchen where
you dine on the scent of pilgrims' marigolds then
backyard to play with your elephant-headed son

Preserve your worshipper Sonal
who in Omkareshwar suggested
I bathe in the Narmada River "for Shiva power"
He was 25 but looked much older
His parents were "finished"
He dressed like people did long before America

"Coming without invitation / Leaving without leave"
wrote Allama Prabhu about you
In the 12th century he had no clue what he would do
when you reveal yourself as the origin of light
He turns your attention
to the leaf that disappears as soon as
"the body grazes without the head"
He sounds like Wittgenstein or my buddy Kit
He wonders what faces look like before people are born

Ganesh your infant son was beheaded by
you in a horrible misunderstanding
brains eyes darling face ashen
Desperate to reverse time
you tore off the nearest available head
an elephant's   and put it onto your son's body

Elephant memory transplanted onto human form
(This is the deity who would grow up to love books)
You adored the recapitated boy and thanks to
one elephant martyr in prehistory's divine evasive chronology
all elephants in India are worshipped today

It's Ganesh's sweet elephant-boyish nature in
family portraits squirming and giggling
as you look stern protective and proud
showing you love him dearly while
like Tony Soprano you keep your weapons within reach
A proud dad you accept your son as he is
When will America's fathers do the same

I remember what Honey told me
dropping me off at the airport: "Now your
holiday is ended. Now you must work."
We were far from the roads of Omkareshwar
where signs read "The Forest Is God's Temple"

> Discontinuous life through continual rotation
> Your singular beauty Shiva
> perpetuates itself in all living things

TO DIONYSUS

IN MEMORY OF ROBERTO CALASSO

My plea to Apollo failed. Hear how
I don't speak in hexameter, the indicator of his possession?
Maybe it's fine and my poems will be good enough.
But not yet. In India, you confronted the Hindu belief
that meters of verse are the cattle of gods. You shook
your head no, and favoring chaos, you declared war on them.
Maybe I need your derangement to pace my breath,
fill my lungs to rupture, honeyed, herbal, scarred. I'm prepared:
I've fought lung ailments, kind of like Kafka and Keats.
At their graves I buried my pencil.
Funny that each had an F.B.—Felice Bauer, meet
Fanny Brawne. I cruise parks and baths for my
own F.B., drinking wine excessively to possess
and ingest another: I'll compromise on metamorphosis.

Olympians gave their bodies to common people—
they wanted to encounter death, so they turned
their asses to our groins. I'd hate to be in a god's position:
immortal, unfeeling, hoping to learn their opposite by
bottoming. Look farther west.
Because San Francisco has no winter,
a perennial spring will gush from your torso:

a viscous liquid like nectar. A vine from Sonoma that chokes trees
and the poor.
If you answer me, I'll raise a statue of you in Dolores Park
where kids fresh out of Stanford get
day drunk on White Claw. They'll lift you into the cloud:
the domain of Apollo, your rival. He'll seethe like an
ants' mound and bow helplessly like he does when mounting
a pubescent boy.
Living flesh won't be transfixed, no,
but data will—immortal, endlessly reckless, almost your double.

ORIGINS OF THE WORLD

Hints of heaven were impossible to inscribe
in early humans who fought thanklessly—
earthlings ignorant of etymology
To capture their existence for the future
they attempted life masks, but I've heard
they were unfit to fill their form
Their material required millennia to
cool and harden—these subjects couldn't be stilled

Poets don't write anymore about the origin of
the world. Why? My guess is
the world stopped recognizing poets' births
so poets stopped addressing the subject
The world asked its other occupants to participate
in its creation instead
Others more agreeable or practical stepped in then
poets forgot the topic, or we became
its undecided satellites

BUCOLIC

I chased her into treehood
   Only my devotion is unchanged
    my naval hair picked of lice while
      from her, it's caterpillar, gypsy moth

      blood filtering
sap sucking
    saliva splashing

My I is not subject but station
  for experience, desire

     bedroom doors   aerial roots

Our transformations accurate   among themselves

THE MARRIAGE OF HELLAGABALUS

It's not a discus or frisbee splitting my face but
   a bull's penis limp on my crown chakra
   Meet Venus in vegan fur, Actaeon with strap-on antlers,
A's outfielder Josh Reddick in dorky briefs and wrestling belt
   As I walk past bonfires to swap vows I think
   these burning branches once were arms, those dead
      leaves hair, these knots weeping sap eyes   Life still
   exhilarates me, my tush crack freshly waxed, tan line
   just right, nostrils a bit crusty from sniffing Viagra and
Jungle Juice, blistering lip befouling imperial purple...
      Across eternity's partitions I say *I do* and switch to solar—
I'm wife to incense-rich blood-bathed versifying Apollo.

Then the reception! Feeling pointlessly flamboyant
I tell bald one-eyed gouty countertenors and women I
swore into the senate *Have a seat*   Hear whoopee cushions
   (history's first) rip from antiquity into your likes
   My whorish honeymoon in summertime snowy heaps, my
      heated seawater pool fogging up San Francisco Bay

TO APOLLO

Licked clean in sun's eye
vision and memory are rivals
Ceiling inscribed with celestial data
gold tesserae   ivy boundary
Will I get my rights?
Is my wandering boy alive?
Heat migrates to bedsheets
a smile breaking along the groin
Sunken chest shines with semen
how the genome limits dictation
This glistening through dew is
the fur of a stag that's escaped
Isn't nature a pulsating wardrobe
Are you inviting or mimicking me?
Will I become a refugee?
The blade reflects a sacrifice's neck
supplicant   anti-cadaverous
a trance in search of an observer
laughing earth

ASCENTS OF ORPHEUS

FOR TORI AMOS

I cling to my wife's coffin
as it speeds to Earth's center
My head bumping 300 bpm
through   geologic eras

An alphabet scratched onto me

      Gutenberg dis-
      continuity

       •

In Hell I sing:

      If my mus-
      Ic is per-
      Verted through tran-
      Script-
      Ion, I'll simply lose
      It.

      No one wants to re-
      Verse your
      System more than
      I.

·

Back on Earth
boys' groins resemble my lyre
With so many eyes on me
I have to put mine somewhere
         a shallow furrow I might not
         return from

·

I'm awake when
a snake swallows my spine
Fragmented I keep creeping

I'm nameless when
Wolfgang Amadeus or
Tori Amos lifts notes from my tongue
Dismembered I keep speaking

·

I learned to play
by imitating nature

I strummed and trilled
to animals and elements
composing me

Wildlife didn't
resemble me
My behavior was theirs
originally

I was only a
stag-headed hunter
a dolphin-tailed swimmer
a lizard-tongued exterminator
a horse-eyed rider

•

My left eye is clenched in
the beak of a migrating ibis
the sun illumining the
underside of its wings

My vision overrun
by joyous
ants and maggots

•

Wildlife running back from extinction
would burn the calluses off my fingers

My right hand severed at the wrist
is nesting four speckled eggs in a pine

•

Looking back at
my wife was
an admission I
doubt
my discipline

Interrogating that
doubt is
the job of
these animals

ANOTHER TRUE ACCOUNT
(THIS TIME ABOUT NOT TALKING TO
THE SUN IN SAN FRANCISCO)

As I typed up that last poem, two guys emerge from the fog
    outside. Oh I know them from my library! It's
the authors of "The Metamorphosis" and *Metamorphoses*.
    To the left, Franz Kafka: stern look, 6' tall, gray suit,
      eyes flickering with spiritual delinquency.
On the right, Ovid: exile-broken body, tunic stiffened by
    Black Sea breeze, elegiac gestures.

The Roman adjusts his tunic and laurel crown:
      "Don't think this is a visit like Apollo
in my *Art of Love*, or how the 20th century
      gives Him no choice but to appear to poets as the sun."
I furtively look toward my library. It's ringing no bells
    though Ovid drops a hint: "He visited an atheist, then
    years later a lapsed Catholic . . . You're stealing
      from me, Kennedy, and from other poets too, passing off
second-rate imitations as dictation from the Muse.
    While your taste is commendable, your thefts are not."

    "We're calling it intertextuality," I say, unnerved
by Franz's icy but boyishly endearing silence. He's shy like me.
(Maybe I should bring up my semester in Prague. . .)

"Ovid, consider how difficult it is to be original, especially
after two millennia in the shade of your laurel crown.
And after Kafka's prophetic bestiary. You've read him?"

"No Latin translation exists." "Oh of course.
Maybe I'll ask Noah to work on one." "Now that Kafka stands
beside me, I see someone who suffered as much as I did
but spiritually, whereas I grieve because I haven't
laid eyes on Rome since my boat left Ostia for my exile.
Consider this visit a compliment. I could be touring
Palatine Hill right now."

"I was there last month! I read my
travel guide but never made sense of all those dreary ruins."
Ovid sighs like he hadn't considered what year it is. I nod
and say, "Exile sounds awful, sure. For me, I feel
estranged with each bit of breaking news.
In my poems, these so-called *second-rate imitations*,
I'm taking the forms of all living things so I can account for
everything. How else can I do that than by
consulting my favorite writers of the distant past?"

Ovid ponders a sec then answers:
"Perhaps you're reading Kafka and me to equip yourself.
That's good. I was going to suggest you step back and
practice my seduction tips, but now I sense
your private sorrow, and your generally good looks,
so all that's for Cupid to sort out.

Instead, here's what we advise (and our books
will agree).

Follow Apollo's
commandment at Delphi: *Know yourself.*
Get your nose out of our books, meet the transience
of your life and identity, its changes. Spot companions
among the forms you'll meet, exchange advice.
Sometimes they'll want money or a sympathetic ear or
to share your bed. Or you'll want to. Or worse,
they'll bore you, misunderstand you, bad mouth your friends
and your clothes—a painful estrangement.

Whatever happens,
synchronize your changes, show care and caution,
keep it lively, various—lend credibility
to your appearances, and defend yourself."

I nod until Ovid's last,
ominous point. I guess it's obvious like all advice, but
that doesn't mean it'll be easy.

Then Kafka clears his throat:
"Regardless of our errors, trust us. We are the Experts,
after all." (Experts?)

I take a peek at my phone—a selfie
might be nice—but then my two guests are gone.
They've disappeared into my confounding microclimate.

GREGOR SAMSA, JR.

Waking this morning I'm a whir of
  scales hooves fins fur paws feathers branches
     and all that passed into extinction (like the long strange
       trip of the naked ape greeting us)
  Wildlife dirties my bedsheets   life scents infusing domestic walls

With feeler tendril limb I examine snout lips incisors beak tongue
  My eyes two globes varying together in size
     registering my room to   each species' necessities

I walk up 24th Street here in San Francisco like my face is
       a flipbook of wildlife portraits, self-generating multiplying
  eluding recognition   changing by your angle of vantage

Made of light or made for its directing
   I try to remain the fissure through which
diverse elusive possibilities/populations approach

In these attitudes remote from matter, time circles back
   to kiss itself   recollect itself for *me*

TREE OF LIFE

In the tree of life I revise my animal body I edit my poem
By unremarked changes creation moves around and within me
Orbits animate nature   nature disbands retreats implodes so that
I name them when I make my first sound
In the tree of life my vantage will change by what species I speak as
my speech not existing for itself but as a branch toward being
a branch one keeps following until another is met or it breaks
dropping me extinct
those roots the inverse image of our branches
When will these distinctions be unneeded
I ask because I doubt I can specify "I" any longer
    Regardless   when I ask my question it will be
    with the same elocution charm desire

LAST UTOPIAN,

moon at day observes the migration of all that precedes and creates
    you:
Castor and Pollux, Nikolai Gogol, David Bowie raised by your
    apotheosis
race orbitless, shaping from out there in exosphere an ear canal
tracing your global travels winters and springs
      Earth is not finished—it's your friends who are finished
      when they give up on Earth and you as lost

You wish to populate the world with serene figures, near-life
    experiences
but you're tired of being Last Utopian—desolated, body-ruined,
in need of a long slow fuck, no place or idea of origin,
slick trail of selves left behind among others cold, noisy, thirsty
Trust thin antennae—hairs along ears' curve, entrance of cave or hive
while you, Last Utopian, are at the mercy of surveillance, and
    absence.
It's unknown what takes the place of loss but it will take place   so
    concentrate
adjust to the constraint of being unable to read future poets now
It's just not possible to read them backward so they greet you where
    you are today

In the desert, red sun (your last light, your relentless seducer) sets on
	western-streaked boulders
SPF 60 and you'll still peel under recollected San Francisco sun
When the security guard in the Valley of Kings invites you
to photograph Osiris's portrait and climb the sarcophagus,
do not photograph Osiris, and do not climb the sarcophagus.
Just don't. Don't trust him.
Apollo the sun burns and peels you because he (unlike some you
	desire) is
aching for your worship
He approaches you in Udaipur, New York, Prague, Rome
smiling like open doors saying no more bedbugs, chlamydia, friends'
air mattresses, jetlag, cocaine hangover, braindead office, bike wreck
	concussion
He brings you humility. You're little more than the eel wriggling
to escape the sizzling wok in a viral cooking video oceanside,
lid rattling over you with scallions and veggies, black-aproned chef
	fumbling
comically for clicks in the merciless algorithm

Enter life elsewhere before life enters yours without your permission:
simple equations, atom clusters, friendships
Ask any atom why it does what it does then
ask a unicorn, selkie, chupacabra, nymph, minotaur
Sense all identity reduced to fragments
—a character from Ovid whose frayed bleeding roots land abroad

But hold on! You are Last Utopian!

Your investigations establish a self while affirming life

like you're Wittgenstein sent as ambassador

from the 21st century to the feet of Shankara in the classroom of
     ego-death

The language of spirit is expressed in prepositions, you say

     Spirit is above, below, next to, and one hopes, within.

In defense of the self, you suggest that joy underlies every living
     thing

once conditions for survival are assured.

          Watch the viral video of dolphin greeting humans

          or the tranquility and delight of mystics

          or the joy of children and dogs

All these are faith's basis—with William Blake and Anthony,

that curly-haired boy of unshakably good cheer met in a Baltimore
     gay bar

His mom said he was happy from the day he was born

—you had been a walking negation then melted before his smile

Remember you've been kissed soft and wet on the lips by Iggy Pop

A sense of self initiates joy of encounter, curiosity, interaction

You hate and love that matter is essential to be

greeted by others astonished   a consolation

It's so California but let's write it:

this sense of self mustn't be extinguished,

it should be named your name which is the transient name of
    anyone

even of those you loathe and risk becoming

You're laid on your back by mushrooms up in Joshua Tree boulders
    February 2021

Delight in identifying with the repertoire of expressions in

Kafka and Chopin—your smile of recognition spans centuries,
    continents!—

It's a language like those not making art but instead living life: I
    mean animals.

Two ravens circle overhead eyeing you for dinner—

they think you're dead when you're emerging from a trance that was

without feeling without content: you met attributeless being,

  the animating force not in the eye but that by which the eye sees

    As Judy Garland sang, *That's entertainment*

You're going slack and gray, face it, at risk of losing these sensations

to which sex can rarely compare though at times it exceeds
    imagination,

and to which Edward Gibbon can rarely compare though

he indicates your decline which is the fall of America taking place in
    you

It was enough when you purchase in that swarmed Kolkata market

the gray-blue shirt that reads LAST UTOPIAN,—

that comma indicates the addressee you were becoming handing
    over your rupees
It's Christmas Eve alone among frantic yet cheerful bottlenecked
    crowds
wearing Santa hats Easter bunny ears devil horns
                every American holiday happening at once

I WOULD BE THERE

among changes
always arriving
not fully comprehending
what shape I'm in
or my stature or thought
These revisions
my instincts struckthrough
contradictory

I don't completely get
these relations
stem and tissue
symmetry and scribble
I liked these lessons
bred in rot
sunk in contagion
behind the sun and its deity
shedding petals and pelt

ACKNOWLEDGMENTS

My deep appreciation to those essential to shaping this book: Suzy Beemer, Bruce Boone, Garrett Caples, Ryan Darley, Jackqueline Frost, Peter Hochschild, Brett Price, Noah Ross, San Francisco Public Library's Interlibrary Loan Department, Adam Sussman, and everyone named within.

Previous incarnations of these poems were published in *Brooklyn Rail*, *Castle Grayskull*, *Local Knowledge*, *Senna Hoy*, and *Vozdukh Magazine*. My thanks to the editors.

Quotations: "THIS IS MY OVIDIAN COURSE": "Heroides" translator, Harold Isbell; "Poems of Exile" translator, Peter Green. "To Shiva": Allama Prabhu translator, H.S. Shivaprakash.

*The state of the world calls out for poetry
to save it.* LAWRENCE FERLINGHETTI

CITY LIGHTS SPOTLIGHT SHINES A LIGHT ON THE WEALTH
OF INNOVATIVE AMERICAN POETRY BEING WRITTEN TODAY.
WE PUBLISH ACCOMPLISHED FIGURES KNOWN IN THE
POETRY COMMUNITY AS WELL AS YOUNG EMERGING POETS,
USING THE CULTURAL VISIBILITY OF CITY LIGHTS TO BRING
THEIR WORK TO A WIDER AUDIENCE. IN DOING SO, WE ALSO
HOPE TO DRAW ATTENTION TO THOSE SMALL PRESSES
PUBLISHING SUCH AUTHORS. WITH CITY LIGHTS SPOTLIGHT,
WE WILL MAINTAIN OUR STANDARD OF INNOVATION AND INCLUSIVENESS
BY PUBLISHING HIGHLY ORIGINAL POETRY
FROM ACROSS THE CULTURAL SPECTRUM, REFLECTING
OUR LONGSTANDING COMMITMENT TO THIS MOST
ANCIENT AND STUBBORNLY ENDURING FORM OF ART.

CITY LIGHTS SPOTLIGHT